table of
contents

friendship paper crafts

friends

SISTERS

family
bonds

Many of our strongest connections are the ties that bind us to family members: our siblings, spouse, parents, grandparents, aunts, uncles, and cousins. Commemorate a very special friendship with a family member by creating a one-of-a-kind scrapbook layout.

my sister

Renee Villalobos-Campa used soft-hue papers to showcase a series of big brother-baby sister photos. Playing off the retro motif of the flower-pattern paper, she cut the pieces into geometric shapes to create a layered background. Journaling blocks printed on quadrilaterals of matted paper jut out from the secondary photos. Renee mimicked the flower pattern to create the large pieced design that contains the title.

Design by Renee Villalobos-Campa

sisters are the best kinds of friends

The strong bond of sisters Jessica and Jaky is evident from the cheek-to-cheek photo that Krista Fernandez selected for this orange-and-pink layout. She hid the journaling on a ribbon-tied tag that slides behind a retro-motif paper. Krista stamped the title with two fonts and heat-embossed the letters. Metal corners accent the photo.

Design by Krista Fernandez

BROTHERS SISTER BROTHERS SIST BROTHERS TER

Always

friends

SIBLINGS

OCTOBER 2003 EVERGREEN COLORADO

56 57 58 59

Even though months and sometimes even years go by without seeing each other, Tom, Carol and Jim remain close siblings and friends. There's always plenty of laughter when the three of them are together.

siblings

Stacy McFadden's photos from a family reunion capture the bond that remains strong between her husband and his siblings, despite the distance that often separates them. Stacy used rustic, textural elements including a wood-grain-pattern paper and fabric swatches of corduroy, muslin, and canvas to represent the rugged Colorado location where the photos were taken. She accented the arrangement of photos with a playful "friends" tab, a three-dimensional sticker, and a bookplate.

Design by Stacy McFadden

my man

Muted brown tones in the textured papers and computer printing accentuate the black-and-white photo of Jennifer Wohlenberg's special guy. For added interest, she wrapped the journaling block and photo mat with lengths of twisted brown fibers and then pulled the two halves of the page together with a strand that stretches across the bottom of the page.

Design by Jennifer Wohlenberg

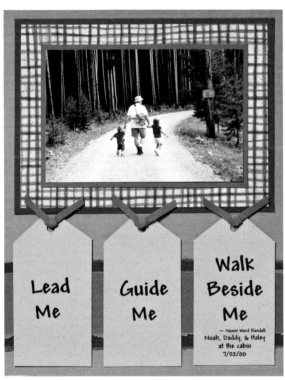

lead me, guide me, walk beside me

Marianne Larsen took this photo during a family fishing expedition at a nearby brook. Then she created this layout as a celebration of her children's best friend, their dad. The tags were created to fit the page space, and the ties are simply thin, knotted strips of card stock. Marianne triple-matted her photo with rust, plaid, and deep blue card stock and created a torn-paper band with more card stock to run behind the tags.

Design by Marianne Larsen

playmates & pals

Blending literary references about youth with weathered elements, Joanna Bolick emphasizes the ageless relationship her father and son share. Joanna added the name and date caption to the photo with an illustration program, computer-printed it, and sanded the edges. She printed the title and journaling on card stock. Patterned paper and a printed transparency complete the bottom portion of the page.

Design by Joanna Bolick

my

Mother

enjoys her morning walks
loves to decorate her house
loves to go shopping
likes entertaining & does a great job at it
is a wonderful & supportive wife to my father
enjoys sewing & knitting
is a wonderful grandmother
loves music & teaches piano, voice, music theory & history
loves the Lord & has been a tremendous example to me
taught me to sew, knit and play piano
is a very loving & caring person
has a wonderful voice & loves to sing
is the best mother and she's also ...

my mother, my friend

While on a day trip to Vancouver Island, Cari Locken seized the opportunity to have special photos taken with her mother. Cari combined the images with a list of the many qualities she cherishes about her mother.

Rickrack and zigzag stitching define vertical and horizontal strips of patterned paper on her layout. Cari's photos, as well as letter stickers, stand out on a machine-stitched mat of dark card stock. Her feature photo was further emphasized with zigzag stitching and a metal frame accented with a button and tags.

Design by Cari Locken

* winter, * spring,

my wish for you...

I want you two to know how important you are to each other. Brothers and sisters need to always be there for each other, even if the rest of the world turns away. As children you are each other's first playmates, but as you grow into adults you will also be each other's best friend.

My wish is for you to love each other, respect each other, and be there for each other. There will be times when you'll be annoyed or mad. It's already begun at a young age. It breaks my heart in a million pieces when I see you fight. I always tell you how special you guys are to each other and how important it is to be nice.

Logan, I want you to watch over Kaylen as she grows. Make sure she stays on the right path and protect her. Realize she will have different opinions, friends, and goals. Respect them and encourage her to do good things in her life. Look after her, but foremost be a friend.

Kaylen, I want you to also look after Logan. He may be older, but we all need someone to help protect and guide us. Realize he wants the best for you, too. Respect the advice he gives you for what it is, in return for his respect, too.

Make each other laugh. Be there when the other is hurt. Do not hit or yell. Respect and support each other. Don't waste a day of your life in anger. Most importantly, be friends.

/ summer, * or fall...

All you have to do is call And I'll be there, yeah, yeah, yeah. You've got a friend.
   —James Taylor

winter, spring, summer, or fall

Inspired by lyrics from a James Taylor song, Lisa Storms encourages her children to love, protect, and befriend each other throughout the seasons of life. Small punched shapes, enhanced with clear embossing powder, embellish the seasonal titles bordering each photo. Repetition of the muted card stock colors in narrow strips gives the poignant design a finished look.

Design by Lisa Storms

discover the moment

It occurred to Andrea Steed that this photo captured the moment when she and her brother Jake had put aside sibling tiffs and became friends. Mounting the photo on folded card stock gave Andrea space to journal about this new phase in their relationship. For the layout, she created dimensional interest using stamped lettering combined with handwriting, engraved metal tags, and glass mosaic tiles framing the photo.

Design by Andrea Steed

sisters

Carrie Colbert knows that she and her sister share a bond as sisters—and as friends. This page features a photo of them, backed by patterned papers in colors that blend with the colors in the photo. Carrie used hand-printed journaling and spelled out "friend" and "sister" in metal tiles. Heart-studded metal corners at the top left and bottom right finish the page.

Design by Carrie Colbert

my brothers, my family, my friends

A simple snapshot of Stacey Sattler with her two brothers allowed her to pay tribute to the trio. Stacey mounted the photo on crumpled card stock and layered that over solid card stock and strips of patterned papers. The title combines handwriting and rub-on letters. Stacey created a tag-style card for each sibling from folded card stock adorned with a cut-out heart, an initial sticker, and a handwritten name. Inside the ribbon-tied cards are lists of personality traits true to each sibling.

Design by Stacey Sattler

pals forever

Alisia, Mandy, and Charla are pals, partners, and—most importantly—sisters. According to Charla, time spent with her sisters is precious and priceless. She cherishes the friendship she has with them and created this layout to document their special bond.

   To give the pages a timeless look, Charla converted color photographs to black-and-white and accented the main photo with flowers cut from the color version. It looks like a hand-colored photo but is created in a fraction of the time.

Design by Charla Campbell

best friends

Erin Roe admits to having "boxes and boxes of photos" from her pre-scrapbooking days. Resigned that she'd never be able to complete a page for every event, she combined many favorite photos of her husband and herself from several celebrations to feature on this layout.

Considering the variations of light and color on each picture, Erin gave the photos a consistent look by cropping them into 2-inch circles and inking the edges. She also cropped, inked, and positioned alphabet circles among the photos to spell the word "friends." She filled the negative space with soft, monochromatic patterned paper and solid card stock, giving the eye a resting point in the design. Alphabet tags, secured with ribbons and brads, complete the title.

Design by Erin Roe

the path of
friendship

It may begin by hanging out in the backyard or school hallways, playing on the same team, or talking for hours on the phone with a favorite buddy. Then distance created by family moves, college stays, or other factors may force a detour. But good friends always get back on track. Sharing—and recording—vacations and major (or minor) life events paves the road to togetherness.

unity

A favorite photo spurred Kate Nelson to delve deep to record the memories behind the scene. She imagined what the girls were seeing, hearing, and feeling physically. She wondered what they might be thinking. Her journaling preserves the essence of the experience, and the matting, paper color, and leaf stamp capture the serenity of the moment.

Design by Kate Nelson

WHEN THE ROAD
LOOKS ROUGH AHEAD

you've got a

F R I E N D

in me

you've got a friend in me

No matter what road these boys' feet travel, their youthful friendship will endure in this page by Jennifer Knewbow. Layers of paper in script, map, and measuring-tape patterns form a strong backdrop for the black-and-white photo. Jennifer stamped a sentiment on kraft paper and inked the edges. The title is a mix of typewriter-key stickers and rubber-stamped letters.

Design by Jennifer Knewbow

That is the best — to laugh with someone because you think the same things are funny.

Brittany

Sami

July 2003

that is the best

On their annual trip to the beach, Jana Millen captured her niece Sami and a friend laughing together and decided to showcase it on this page.

Using photo-editing software, Jana printed the photograph in black-and-white and added a quote at the bottom in pink. She left a narrow white border around the photo when trimming it. A torn pastel-striped paper is adhered to a beige background. The ribbon embellishment was made by folding one ribbon end around a metal ring, poking a hole through both layers of the ribbon, and inserting a mini brad to secure. After repeating the process for the other side of the ring, Jana hung two metal-rim tags from the ring with embroidery floss and adhered the ribbon ends to the back of the page.

Design by Jana Millen

true friends

When family friends announced they would be moving away, the news was especially hard on Diana Hudson's daughter Sydney and her soon-to-be-leaving friend Rachel. Diana found the creation of this special layout to be therapeutic, and she hopes the girls will always treasure the value of true friendship.

Diana used reproduction vintage postcard-print paper to symbolize the physical distance between the two girls. She machine-stitched strips of torn postcard-print paper to the cranberry handmade paper and added heart-pattern paper on top. She aged the edges of the papers and the alphabet letters with brown ink. The photo is mounted on a flap—secured with a clasp—to reveal journaling underneath. Diana also replicated the heart tag printed on the postcard paper by combining two tag templates, aging the edges with brown ink, and satin-stitching a heart on it.

Design by Diana Hudson

treasure good friends

The brother of Lindsay Teague's boyfriend has many friends, which Lindsay attributes to his loyalty. When many of Jason's closest friends were groomsmen at a friend's wedding, Lindsay jumped at the opportunity to photograph them all together.

She chose a soft green color palette to complement the black-and-white group photos and used green mesh to create a textural frame around the gray card stock background. The photo mat and torn strip at the bottom of the page were created from the same patterned green paper, and black-and-white print paper creates visual separation for the title and photo layers. To allow the wire title to stand out against the paint swatch background, Lindsay sanded a large spot off the center of the swatch. She also lightly sanded the small photos to create a faded border around the subjects. Alphabet stickers and black label tape complete the title and captions, and a black tag containing journaling tucks behind the main photo.

Design by Lindsay Teague

friends

When Melissa Inman was planning her wedding, she spent many hours figuring out what each member of the bridal party would wear. She scoured magazines for ideas, pored over pattern books, and hunted high and low for the perfect fabrics. She chose autumn hues for the September ceremony and had each of the bridal party ensembles custom-made—right down to the ties the groomsmen wore.

So when it came time to scrapbook her photos and memories, she wanted a way to include the colors and fabrics that had been so important to the event, while keeping the focus on the image. In this layout, Melissa matted the title block with a swatch of the plaid fabric used in the groomsmen's ties and her husband's vest. She frayed the edges slightly for a soft look.

Design by Melissa Inman

Things I've learned from Shelley:

it's possible to make real-life friends through the internet

optimism is contagious

sweet people do exist

procrastination is an art form

there is no such thing as 'too much' ribbon

things i've learned from shelley

Introduced through online scrapbooking communities, Stacey Sattler finally met her friend Shelley face-to-face about two years ago. Since then, Stacey and Shelley have had many opportunities to develop their friendship by teaching together and meeting at scrapbooking events. Stacey's layout reflects on the many things she has learned from her treasured friend.

Stacey packed a punch of color into a small area by stitching a border from several styles of patterned paper, alternating the types of stitches and using colored thread for extra impact. Simple embellishments pull color into the rest of the page and allow Stacey's solo photograph to shine.

Design by Stacey Sattler

my music

This layout is a tribute to Alison Beachem's love of music and how her college roommates exposed her to different styles, forever changing her music tastes. Alison cleverly hid journaling about musical groups and albums under the smaller photo and she made the miniature album covers by printing scanned and reduced CD covers. Each cover lifts to reveal her writing.

Design by Alison Beachem

pen pals

United by a love of scrapbooking but divided by the ocean, Olga Waywood-Joyce of Canada and Annette Knutsen of Norway developed a friendship after meeting through an online scrapbooking community. As their own relationship progressed, Olga and Annette encouraged their children to become pen pals and learn about each other's home country.

Olga found inspiration for her layout in the color schemes of the Canadian and Norwegian flags. A slender string-closure envelope stands in contrast to primary-color card stock and provides a clever mat for her title and photo of her daughter's pen pals. Olga replicated a postmark, positioned near authentic postage, by printing her text in reverse onto a laser transparency. The transparency left the ink wet enough to be transferred to the envelope, giving it a worn effect. Rubber-stamped lettering completes the postmark outline.

Design by Olga Waywood-Joyce

ice hockey rocks

Friendships often develop when children play on a team and experience together the thrill of a win … and the agony of defeat. Textured paper creates an interesting backdrop for this page focusing on a young hockey team, and the deep red and black papers enhance the colors in the photos. Kathleen Paneitz labeled each photo with strips of paper either adhered to the photo or clipped on. Accents include photos of hockey sticks and puck, as well as a stamped metal frame around a special photo. Shoelaces stretched across the left page hold a round metal-rim tag embellished with hockey skate stickers. The stickers were originally roller skates, but Kathleen snipped off the wheels and replaced them with silver blades.

Design by Kathleen Paneitz

paradise with friends

Krista Fernandez and two of her friends had such a great time together in Hawaii that she wanted to create a layout that conveyed the tropical fun they shared. Guided by the clothing colors in the photo of the happy trio, Krista chose complementary paper and embellishments to unify the various page elements. She created a unique tag accent by tearing out the paper center from a rectangular metal-rim tag, fastening black ribbon to it, and mounting it on a piece of sheer purple gingham ribbon. She then placed a clear acrylic word and a round word cutout inside the tag frame. Another acrylic word and a metal flower accent tied with gingham ribbon balance the page.

Design by Krista Fernandez

highlights with jen wen my friend

Alison Beachem designed this page to document a long-lasting friendship. "My friend Jennifer and I have been friends since we were both 8 years old," Alison says. "We met at Sunday school and although we weren't close friends growing up, we knew much about each other from our after-church play dates at each other's houses."

Once the two began attending the same high school, they became much closer. And when Alison went away to college, the two became best friends. Since then, the two have been through much—both good times and bad. The layout documents their shared milestones through journaling blocks printed on strips of vellum, which have had their edges torn and chalked. Each block is accented with a brass mini brad, as are the date tags she cut from patterned card stock. The title was made by reverse-printing the text on card stock and cutting out the letters with a craft knife. The title reflects the way Alison and Jennifer have signed cards since high school: "Jen Wen" and "Al Pal."

Alison chose the photo of the pair on the slopes as the focal point of this layout because she says it "really represents the two of us together. The photo is of us in Utah skiing on a trip we took without our husbands and kids. We only skied one day, but we had a great time and this is one of my favorite pictures of the two of us."

Design by Alison Beachem

 brian and sage

The clean lines of modern designs allow for plenty of experimentation. Although Vivian Smith could have paired her lake picture with a water-theme page, she instead found inspiration in a dress from the 1960s designed by Yves Saint Laurent. She used a straightedge and craft knife to cut the black lines and tucked rectangles of yellow, blue, and red beneath the three cross sections.

Design by Vivian Smith

brian & sage

Alan, Cindy, & Brian came to visit this summer for about 10days. We did a lot of traveling together to local sites like Drumheller, Banff, Lake Louise (this photo was taken here), & Kananaskis. We were hoping Brian & Sage would hit it off, & we were lucky that for the most part they did. Brian is really into trains & brought much of his "Thomas the Tank" train set with him. He just couldn't understand why Sage didn't share the same enthusiasm for trains. Summer, 2003

DREAMS and **PRAYERS...** from my summer with JEFF 1997

Dreaming of traveling the world.

Dreaming of him finally giving in and liking country music.

Dreaming of going into space... as the first married astronauts.

Dreaming of our colleges being closer together.

Praying for each other's families.

Dreaming of UK & Purdue meeting in a basketball showdown.

Dreaming of owning a boat.

Praying for a household of kids someday.

Praying to be good parents someday.

Jeff and I had a wonderful summer together in 1997. We met at P&G where we interned in the same division. We quickly became close friends. We used to sit and talk about our dreams, and shared our prayers. I'll never forget those talks.
In 1998, Jeff was diagnosed with brain cancer, and fought a long, brave fight. However, in February 2001, he left us to go to heaven. I look forward to seeing him there someday. In the meantime, I continue to pray and dream...

JEFF EPPERSON
March 26, 1974 – February 9, 2001

dreams and prayers

When Jeff, Jennifer Ditz's boyfriend, passed away after a long fight with brain cancer, she decided to construct a layout in his honor, documenting the relationship. "I wanted to do something that focused on the positives and would continually remind me of the wonderful times I had with Jeff," Jennifer says. "When I think about Jeff, I remember the incredible conversations we had. So, I decided to capture them in this layout. Just some random thoughts that I never want to forget."

Jennifer chose warm, inviting colors for the layout, working with rubber stamps and sepia-tone ink to give it a subdued sophistication. For the title block, she layered two pieces of torn card stock, embossing the torn edges with gold enamel, and mirrored the technique on the computer-printed journaling block. She used more gold enamel embossing powder to create the "dreams" part of her title, melting the powder and stamping into the surface while still soft.

Design by Jennifer Ditz

a new season, a new friendship

When Stacy Yoder took her daughter to the pumpkin patch, it was not only the start of the autumn season but the start of a new friendship as well. Even as she took these photos of Lauren and her newfound friend, Kayla, Stacy could feel the bond between them growing.

Stacy's colorful layout showcases an oversize photograph that instantly draws the eye to her subjects. Her title, a combination of stamped and hand-cut letters, balances the image. A greeting card template was altered to house a supporting photo of the girls. Stacy used a variety of embellishments to fill each window of the heat-embossed plastic frame, carrying out the theme of the new friendship.

Design by Stacy Yoder

falling into friendship

A breathtaking fall vista provides the color palette for this page filled with warm hues and journaling about the beginning of a friendship. Leaf-border stickers layered underneath, rather than over, the title block and photo mats complement the scheme.

Design by Cori Dahmen

friends

This simple layout makes the point that these four smiling girls are the best of friends. Daniela Berkhout chose a dark background of olive green and a black floral pattern to show off the grouping of friends. Buttons attach the strip of black card stock on which she stamped the girls' names. The alphabet stickers spelling "friends" were lightly sanded before they were applied to the page.

Design by Daniela Berkhout

chit chat chit chat chit chat chit chat chit chat chit chat
chit chat chit chat chit chat chit chat chit chat chit chat
chit chat chit chat chit chat chit chat chit chat chit chat

It's called a telephone but for the past few years it appears to have become Courtney's life line. It is indeed the line that keeps her connected to her friends and what's happening and where it's at and who's who and what's what and that's that and chit chat and see ya later. On week-ends things definitely escalate with one call after another, from one source or another keeping her informed of where it's at and who's who and what's what and that's that and chit chat and see ya later. The rest of us can often be heard saying, Court the phone is for you or has anyone seen Court or can someone tell Court to get the phone or it's for Court or I'm not answering that because it's for Court. May 2003

chit chat

When the phone rings at Angie Cramer's house, chances are that it's for her daughter Courtney. To document this chatty "friendly" phase of Courtney's life, Angie created this bright page. She computer-printed three lines of "chit chat" across the top of the background paper in olive green, orange, and black ink. Next Angie matted a photo of Courtney on the phone holding another teenage staple—a bottle of hair spray—with white card stock, leaving a thin border on all sides. To keep the elements organized, Angie crafted a color-block background in shades of green and rust, leaving thin white margins between the pieces. Flowers snipped from an old greeting card serve as embellishments, the middle one highlighted by a checkered die-cut frame.

Design by Angie Cramer

live laugh play together

Buddies
Alex & Sam

This is my buddy
This is my Friend
We're stickin' together
clear til the end.

Fall 2002

buddies

Sherrill Ghilardi Pierre created this textured layout to showcase the special friendship between her nephew Sam and his friend Alex. To make the background paper, she roughly brushed artist's cement over half of a piece of white card stock to give it a stuccolike appearance, and she covered the unpainted side of the card stock with torn vellum and striped paper. Smaller pieces of torn vellum were printed with the title and adhered to an arch cut from corrugated cardboard. She placed word beads onto wire earring hoops and strung them together with green fiber. A slide mount covered with green textured paper creates the frame around the word "together."

Design by Sherrill Ghilardi Pierre

celebrating friendship

Whether it's to observe a birthday or a holiday, or just for the fun of getting together, any event is better when you're surrounded by friends.

ingredients for thanksgiving dinner

Turkey, mashed potatoes, and gravy aren't the only ingredients necessary for the perfect Thanksgiving dinner. Nichol Magouirk constructed this layout to document other essentials.

Smudging with brown ink toned down the white card stock she used to make the photo mats and captions. Her tags list ingredients, guests, and the menu, all accented by twisted wire, fibers, or hemp cord. Nicole kept most matting simple to focus on the photos, but she opted for a bit of creativity on the left page. One photo rests on top of the vellum border and another beneath with a window cut to reveal the subject.

Design by Nichol Magouirk

a sweet beginning

After receiving an indoor s'more maker for Christmas, Sydney Hudson immediately made plans to include the gift in a New Year's Eve celebration. Sydney orchestrated every detail, down to the moment the s'mores would be made: midnight, of course!

To embellish and separate the space on the layout, Diana Hudson punched squares of card stock in rich, warm shades and used a corner rounder to soften each one. To include more photos on the page, she cut up the index sheet provided with the prints and included miniature photographs paired with rub-on messages.

Design by Diana Hudson

a sweet beginning
new year's eve 2003

10 · 9 · 8 ·

finally!

yummy

Sydney, our resident social director, planned every detail of New Year's Eve this year. She planned to make s'mores, a treat reserved for special occasions, with her friends as soon as the ball dropped in Times Square – on NYC time, of course! Her dessert was such a success, I think this could be the beginning of a new tradition.

birthday party

GUEST OF HONOR

From left to right:

Cousin Kaylen, Uncle Terry, Daddy, Zoe, Uncle Daniel, Grandpa Deibler, you, GG Deibler, Duelli, Aunt Lisa, GG Deibler, Lala, cousin Logan, Mommy

Just some snapshots of your family enjoying your first birthday party. Although they could not be there, Grandma and Grandpa Roe, Uncle Dave, Unlce Phil and Aunt Sarah called during your party to wish you a happy birthday.

guests

This first birthday party commemoration features a snapshot of each of the party guests, including the guest of honor. Designer Erin Roe says, "When I really love the style of a letter sticker but can't find it in the color I need, I improvise by turning it into an exercise in relief stamping." She places the letter sticker on the paper, stamps over it with a solid shape stamp, and then removes the inked sticker with tweezers to reveal a white letter.

Design by Erin Roe

butterfly birthday

This graceful page by Cheryl McMurray features the flight of the "butterflies" attending her daughter's birthday party. Cheryl used vellum to emboss butterfly images and tipped the edges with a silver glitter gel pen. She also embossed and cut out letters for the title, dressing them up with more glitter gel pen accents and an eyelet in each word.

Design by Cheryl McMurray

mary kate's 5th birthday bash

Fitting all of her daughter's best birthday photos on one layout was a challenge for Sarah Ackerman-Hale. Her solution was to create a highlights layout that shows the best moments and pictures. She used a square punch to crop the photos of the birthday girl and her guests into a manageable size and placed them as accents on the tag embellishments she used on both pages. Because the party was at a farm, Sarah opted for a rustic look for the spread. By utilizing a collage style, she could incorporate lots of colors, textures, and photos. A small hinged book also allowed Sarah a bit more room for photos and captions.

Design by Sarah Ackerman-Hale

good lickin'

Charla Campbell's colorful layout brings a sweet smile to even sticky lips. Raggedy Ann and Andy iron-on embellishments echo the lollipop party treats and frame the hand-written title. Charla's hand-stitching and torn card stock mats add to the homespun appeal.

Design by Charla Campbell

good **Lickin'**

What a fun time Brittany and Kayla had at Garrett's 1st birthday party! They both got a lollipop. It was the first time Kayla ever had one, she loved it!

li'l punkins

Seasonal stickers make quick work out of this Halloween page by Laura Krumpholz. The bottom border looks like multiple layers but is actually one piece. Additional stickers accent the party photo captions and spell out the title.

Design by Laura Krumpholz

par-tea

In a layout fit for a little princess, Lori Bergmann added sparkle and fluff to suit the tone of her daughter Ashley's birthday party. Colorful rhinestones and a golden paper border frame the photos and highlight the golden title, and a feather "boa" matches the finery worn to the royal party.

Design by Lori Bergmann

girls' night out

Candid photos taken at a neighborhood gathering didn't all turn out to be picture-perfect. Jennifer Blackham solved the problem of less-than-ideal shots by cutting each of the 20 photos into small squares. She used only the parts of the photos she liked to create a mosaic featuring each of the attendees and sharing snippets of the evening's action.

Design by Jennifer Blackham

girls
July 17, 2001
Night Out

The women of the neighborhood gathered at the Maxfield home for a delicious Dutch Oven dinner. Lots of chatting & food made it a great evening to get to know each other better. Were you there?

happy new year

Even if the party doesn't last until midnight, a New Year's Eve party-theme layout can incorporate the famous ball dropping at Times Square. Erin Terrell put together this countdown page with stacked tags finished with silver number stickers and fastened with a shiny silver brad. The facing page is a giant pocket holding predictions, resolutions, and memories of a fun celebration with friends.

Design by Erin Terrell

it's all about ...

On this layout by Anita Matejka, melt-art frames draw attention to each significant element of her daughter's birthday party. Anita used a small gold frame to create a mold from two-part silicone molding putty designed to be used for melt art. She then filled the mold with liquefied colored glue sticks and added metallic rub-ons to the frames once they were cool. The featured photos were scanned, edited, and printed in black-and-white, and color versions of the photos were set in the frames. The highlighted photos are mounted on coordinating papers, which form pockets to hold journaling about each of the party's features: gifts, crafts, decorations, cake, and, of course, friends.

Design by Anita Matejka

outdoor fun with friends

When taking off to enjoy the great outdoors, it's a natural to grab a pal—or two or three— to go along for the ride.

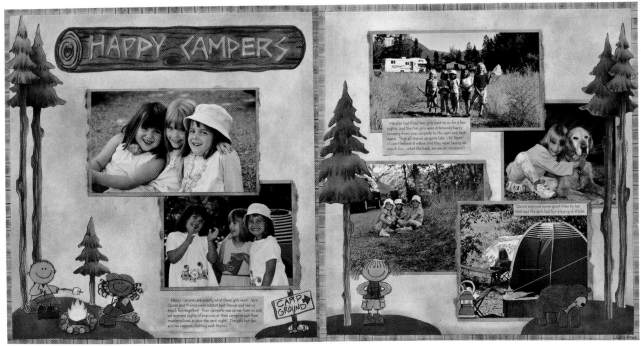

- **happy campers**
- A camping trip with Amy van Engelen's daughter Quinn became even more enjoyable when Quinn formed an instant friendship with two girls from a nearby campsite. The three girls then befriended several more girls at the campground, and they quickly became a pack of happy campers.
-     To remember the friends Quinn made during their stay, Amy used stickers to re-create some of their happy campfire and sightseeing times. For the title, Amy scanned and enlarged a log sticker, printing it out on her color printer.
- Design by Amy van Engelen

boys in the hood

There's plenty of fun on 23rd Street, as these wild and crazy boys can attest! To document their antics, Polly Maly designed a mini book to hold photos and journaling. She created the blocked background by stitching along the perimeter of squares of card stock, inking the edges, and mounting them on a sheet in the same color. The book is made by machine-stitching strips of card stock to a front cover, cutting pages slightly smaller than the cover (Polly's cover is 6×12 inches and her inside pages are 6×11½ inches), and creasing the book down the middle. She punched holes in the fold and threaded a ribbon through to bind the book.

Design by Polly Maly

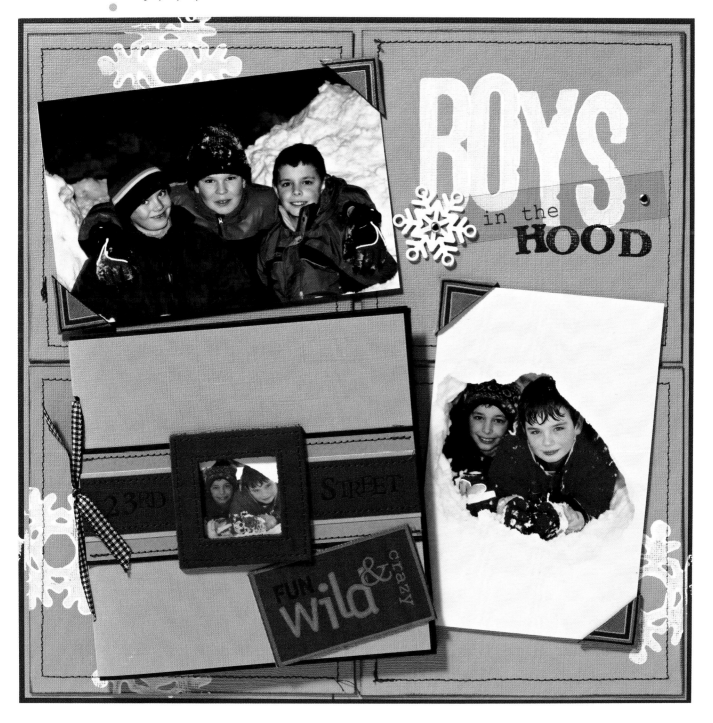

There is a large variety of sizes and age difference in this group of cousins, but time spent together is, no doubt about it, great fun. Late summers in California are generally HOT! Large, open fields and hills of grass are an open invitation for lots of running, chasing, falling down and rolling around – good, sweaty fun. For relief, drink lots of water and when over-heated and red in the face, head for the shade of the really big trees and collapse on the cool summer grass.

Mike, Ethan, Tom, Josh and Tanner

2003

overheated

Roughhousing with "the guys" requires some cool-down time, as these energetic boys found. Helen Naylor captured the moment with a fun title that mixes letters torn from patterned paper, stamped with paint, stamped with bleach, or in the form of stickers. She printed her journaling on the patterned paper and used staples to attach the date strip.

Design by Helen Naylor

skate

Vivian Smith chose a simple design for this spread about a skating excursion with friends one winter morning. The main picture was shot with a polarizing filter on her camera to keep the snow from overpowering the photo. She scanned the other photos, colored them using photo-editing software, and resized them to fit into her design. Small squares in coordinating colors finish the pages at the outer edges.

Design by Vivian Smith

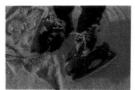

During our 2001 Christmas break, I decided to go for a morning skate with Jonathan & Sharon across the lake between our two cabins. It was really a magical feeling as there was a thin layer of undisturbed snow across the lake & everything was still & sparkling. No one else was around. About ¾ of the way across the lake, one of Jonathan's skates, shoe portion & all, broke apart & fell of his foot. He continued to skate on one leg, but the other skate did the same thing (see photo to left). It was bizarre. The skates were old & I guess the plastic couldn't take the strain in the cold morning. Luckily, Jonathan had brought his shoes with him in his pack, but it did slow our trip down.

December, 2001

exploring nature

This layout captures the excitement of an outing to a natural setting. Lori Bergmann included images of natural wonders viewed during the day at the park: a dragonfly, butterflies, plants, and a bird's nest with eggs. Her photos capture the joys of hiking through the prairie, stopping for a rest near the stream, and eating s'mores at sunset. The s'mores shot is actually two photos carefully aligned and matted as one. The pattern is on *page 62*.

Design by Lori Bergmann

The handwritten journaling on the page reads:

We had such a GREAT ski trip in 2001! We went over Kyle's school break so he was able to join us. The day of this picture we all went to The Canyons... we also got Tere's hubby Dave + his friends visiting from Ohio to join us. It was so nice having a big group! Turns out this was our only photo of us all since the developer ruined 3 rolls of my film!

pile up

This group of snow bunnies piled up for a photo on a Colorado ski trip. White embossing paste gives a snowbound look to Sara Tumpane's wintry layout. To make the title, she cut the computer-printed letters out of white card stock, then painted embossing paste thinned with a bit of crystal lacquer on the letters, let them air-dry, and glued them to the page. For the snow at the bottom of the page, Sara brushed on several layers of paste to achieve the look and thickness she wanted.

Design by Sara Tumpane

nothing is worth more than this day

There's nothing better than spending a hot summer day splashing in the pool with a friend. Shannon Landen showcased one such day in a layout using fabric to mat the photos and journaling box, as well as to create accents. The water, flowers, and sun's rays are made from rectangular strips of fabric rolled on the diagonal. Shannon molded the strips into the desired shapes and used liquid adhesive to secure them to the pages. She finished the flowers by stitching bright yellow buttons to the centers with embroidery floss.

Design by Shannon Landen

my paddling days

With sand as her scrapbooking theme, Arlene Santos experimented with textures. Her pages deliver an exciting and eclectic mix—layers of torn papers, metal sun-worshipper motifs, and corrugated papers are topped with a fabulous foreground of overlapping spirals, made using a spiral paper punch.

Design by Arlene Santos

fairfield mustangs lacrosse

Sara Tumpane featured her son Kyle in action at a high school lacrosse game. To complement the photos, Sara molded polymer clay into a miniature lacrosse stick and several balls. Mesh drywall tape positioned behind the clay frame forms the net of the stick. The flattened balls were adhered around the photos to give the feeling of movement and to balance the layout.

Design by Sara Tumpane

mt. lemmon snow

Darcy Christensen used die-cut snowflakes in a silver metallic paper and silver eyelets to accent the title and journaling blocks on this layout. She made her own patterned paper for the top half of the page, drawing snowflakes on white card stock using color pencils. The alphabet pattern is on pages 62–63.

Design by Darcy Christensen

starry night

When Sarah Champion sat down to record her memories of an outing with friends, she opted for a playful-yet-sophisticated design with subtle embellishments. Sarah used a patterned vellum for the background and several of the star accents and designed her own lettering style for the hand-cut title.

Design by Sarah Champion

pet
pals

If you are head-over-paws for your animal friends, you'll want to capture them permanently on your scrapbook pages.

adorable is my middle name

As soon as Toni and Tom Holoubek saw Chubby, they fell in love with him and welcomed him into the family. But when Toni's allergies grew more severe during pregnancy, they decided it would be best if Chubby went back to the humane society. He was adopted by another family, but the Holoubeks will always remember him as part of their family.

Toni layered vellum and photos on top of color-block background paper. To break all the right angles, she added rub-on circles and stamped her title on top of them. Black chalk darkens the small tags, making them blend in with the rest of the layout.

Design by Toni Holoubek

thomas paulding

Melanie Bauer knew she would have plenty of quiet nights ahead of her while her husband was in medical school, so she adopted a cat from the local humane society. Melanie says that life has changed for the better since Thomas came into their home.

Melanie altered the appearance of the heart charm and eyelet by embossing them in gold to match the warm tones of the paper and the photo.

She covered the slide mount with coordinating patterned paper and looped fibers around its sides. Melanie journaled on striped paper, which she trimmed to fit around the stripes in her background paper. Alphabet stickers add interest to the beginning of the journaling, the title, and the inside of the slide mount.

Design by Melanie Bauer

THOMAS STARTED OUT AS A BIRTHDAY GIFT FROM ANDY, BUT SOON BECAME SO MUCH MORE. HE'S ALWAYS THERE TO GREET ME AT THE DOOR WHETHER I'VE BEEN AWAY FOR THE DAY OR FOR THE WEEK. HE'S MY SCRAPBOOK BUDDY AND SPENDS MANY EVENINGS IN MY CRAFT ROOM WITH ME. THE BEST PART ABOUT HAVING THOMAS IS THAT I HAVE SOMEONE TO KEEP ME COMPANY WHEN ANDY IS ON CAMPUS OR STUDYING AND SOMEONE TO SHARE MY NIGHTLY BOWL OF ICE CREAM! HE GETS HIS OWN BOWL THOUGH!

THOMAS PAULDING

AND EVEN THOUGH HE ATTACKS MY FEET AT BEDTIME, HE'S OFTEN FOUND SLEEPING IN WITH ME AT THE END OF THE BED NEARLY EVERY SATURDAY MORNING.

JUL 2 2 2003

itty bitty kitty

Lucky, a darling little kitten, takes center stage in this layout by Shannon Landen. Thin strips of patterned paper form the mat behind the small photo as well as accent the title block and main photo. Shannon also used a scrap of tan card stock from which circles had been punched and placed different shades of blue paper behind the openings for an easy border.

Design by Shannon Landen

come out and play

Ginger is a playful dog, but when left outside she loves to sit by the door and watch the activity inside the house. Owner Angie Cramer saw Ginger sitting in the doorway and felt Ginger was saying, "Come out and play!" Since Ginger's favorite toy is a ball, Angie used a large circle punch to create the title circles and rotated each one for a sense of motion—like a ball rolling. To match Ginger's fur, Angie chose tan papers and added fibers and mesh for an outdoorsy feel.

Design by Angie Cramer

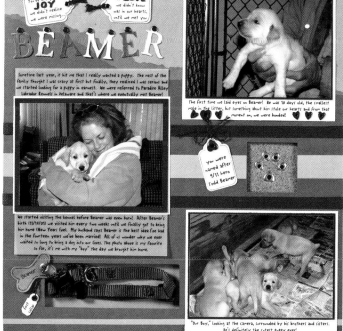

beamer

When Kathleen Paneitz's best friend, Linda, decided to adopt an adorable Labrador, Kathleen offered to make a scrapbook page to document the start of the friendship between the dog and owner.

"She has never had any kind of pet the whole time I've known her. She always thought they were too much work. Then, out of the blue, she decided last year that she wanted a puppy. Now that she has him, you'd think she had loved dogs her whole life. She calls him 'her boy' and bought a king-size bed so he could sleep with her. He's the most pampered dog I've met in a while," Kathleen says.

Kathleen crafted her page background from torn and layered sheets of card stock, strips of light blue card stock in two widths, and lengths of ribbon. After adding matted photos, vellum journaling blocks, and a title of metal letters that dangle from colored brads, she backed the layout with a piece of foam-core board. She cut windows in the layout and foam core, then placed card stock behind the openings, securing Beamer's puppy collar in one opening and fashioning an eyelet paw print set in cork in the other. As a finishing touch, she designed a dog bone name tag for the collar, embossing the piece with silver powder and connecting it to the collar with a red chain.

Design by Kathleen Paneitz

chance

Cindy Johnson says it seemed as if her golden retriever Chance grew up overnight. She treasures these "baby" photos and showcased them in a monochromatic layout in shades of olive green. The background is card stock and torn patterned paper in matching shades. She used a paint swatch as a mat for the large photo. Metal letters spell "Chance," and her journaling swirls above the small photo. The "grow" sticker bridges the black-and-white image to the green background.

Design by Cindy Johnson

smiling, happy faces that i adore always

Smiles fill this page of photos featuring Butterball's and Janae's faces. To use a variety of shots, Kathleen Paneitz included a negative-strip print and cropped detail shots of her daughter and her dog to fit in the clear openings. Photo flips create a hinged flap, perfect for stashing journaling underneath.

Design by Kathleen Paneitz

seven

When naming their dog, the Kyle family made a logical choice. Born as the seventh puppy of the litter, the name Seven seemed only natural. But not until recently did Seven's name have even more significance—when he surprisingly survived being hit by a car without a single injury. Everyone declared that Seven must have seven lives.

As a tribute to their faithful companion, Tracy Kyle snapped this close-up photo of Seven's face, capturing his expressive eyes. She attached the enlarged image to the corner of the page and used random squares cut from a variety of patterned papers to fill the rest of the background. Tracy stitched some squares together with embroidery floss and dressed up others with painted wood numbers, bottle caps, and even a game piece, each one emblazoned with the number seven.

Design by Tracy Kyle

Companion

May 28, 2004
Today was a really rotten, terrible, no good day. It started out like any other day, I got the kids ready for school and we walked there with Seven. Seven and I came home, and I put her in backyard. Within seconds I saw her jump over the fence and start running back towards the school. I grabbed the leash and ran to get her. As I came around the corner, I saw a car coming down the road in front of the school. I held my breath as I heard a terrible thud as the car hit Seven. I cannot explain how sad I felt when I saw her laying there on the ground. Someone offered me a ride and we picked up Seven and took her to the vet. Amazingly, there was absolutely nothing wrong with Seven. The vet was very surprised too and said that she must have seven lives. We are very lucky that Seven is still alive!

SEVEN

bathing patsy

Lee Anne Russell's children decided to give Patsy, their dog, a much-needed bath.

Lee Anne wanted the patterned blue paper to have a gray look so it would coordinate with Patsy's fur. To accomplish this, she shaded the edges of each photo mat or strip with black chalk. She also wanted to emphasize how messy the dog-washing task is, so she enlarged the photo of Patsy shaking. A creative treatment gives the title its charm. To make it, Lee Anne reverse-printed the title, cut it out, and again used the black chalk to darken the edges.

Design by Lee Anne Russell

first puppy

Gina Cabrera loves this photo of her son Peyton playing with his puppy on a sunny day. The two are the best of friends, and Gina feels that this photo is a perfect representation of their relationship.

Gina created this layout on her computer. Starting with an 8½×11-inch file with a landscape orientation, she created a brown and blue background. A canvas effect added texture. Next, Gina layered the photo over the background, then added journaling and the title. To make the metal tag and eyelet, she started with a thick circle and applied a metal effect. To complete the tag, Gina filled the middle of the circle with white and used clip art to add the paw print.

Design by Gina Cabrera

100%
GOOD
99%
OF THE
TIME

" Bonnie, you must fight the urge to dig holes in the yard. You can't go around doing whatever you want to do. It's just not right. You cannot pee on the carpet in your master's new house. How many times do I have to tell you! In case you forget what a conscience is, I have included a definition for your review... and remember...

ALWAYS LET YOUR CONSCIENCE BE YOUR GUIDE!"

Conscience (?). n. [F. *conscience*, fr. l. *conscientia*, fr. *consciens*, p.pr. of *conscire* to know, to be conscious; *con-* + *scire* to know. See Science.] 1. Knowledge of one's own thoughts or actions; consciousness. 2. The faculty, power, or inward principle which decides as to the character of one's own actions, purposes, and affections, warning against and condemning that which is wrong, and approving and prompting to that which is right; the moral faculty passing judgment on one's self; the moral sense.

100% good 99% of the time

When Mary Ann Wise's children looked at this ultra-close shot of their dog Bonnie staring at a grasshopper, they likened it to Bonnie talking to Jiminy Cricket. They imagined that the bug was lecturing Bonnie about all the bad things she had done. Inspired by her kids' creative scenario, Mary Ann wrote the journaling in quotations, as if the little bug had actually spoken those words.

Brown papers create an L-shape border around the enlarged photo. The title and journaling are printed on tan card stock, and accent pieces of polka-dot as well as animal-print papers highlight the areas of interest on the page. Mary Ann embossed a small round tag with copper powder and topped it with a tiny paw charm.

Design by Mary Ann Wise

Benjamin and his friend Derek found this grass snake up at the lake last Summer. Madalynn could not wait to see it. The boys brought the snake up to the deck and Maddy ran right over to them so she could get an up close and personal look at it. All I could do was grab the camera to get some photos of Madalynn with her new friend. She tried to hold this snake, she gave the snake a hug and she even gave the snake a big old kiss. It is amazing to me how she had absolutely no fear of the snake. I guess she will not be afraid of snakes until somebody gives her a reason to fear them. Hopefully she doesn't hear her own Mom when I see a snake!! I cannot stand them and run the other way! Unless, I have a camera in my hand and am taking photos of our daughter meeting a snake for the first time. I can put my own fears aside for that!! Summer 2002 Madalynn 2 years old

snake

Debbie Kuehl's son found a snake that soon had her daughter Maddy enchanted. Maddy couldn't stop playing with it, and even Debbie put her reptile fears aside long enough to take a few fantastic shots of the event.

Bubble-texture paper, which lends a snakelike appearance, serves as an oversize mat for the main photo and title. To accentuate the paper's texture, Debbie rubbed black chalk over the surface. Smaller photos are backed with black card stock, and the vellum-printed journaling is layered behind the photo. Flat-top eyelets and green fibers give the page added interest.

Design by Debbie Kuehl

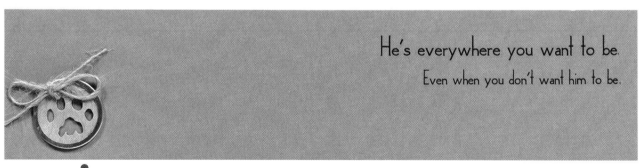

He's everywhere you want to be.

Even when you don't want him to be.

he's everywhere you want to be

A popular credit card slogan inspired Heather Melzer to create this page about her Old English sheepdog, Sebastian. She describes him as a loving dog who needs attention, and because it always feels like he's in the way, Heather enlarged this close-up to exaggerate her point. Strips of of blue and tan card stock accent the oversize photo. A paw punched out of a metal-rim tag is embellished with a small twine bow and adhered in the lower left corner.

Design by Heather Melzer

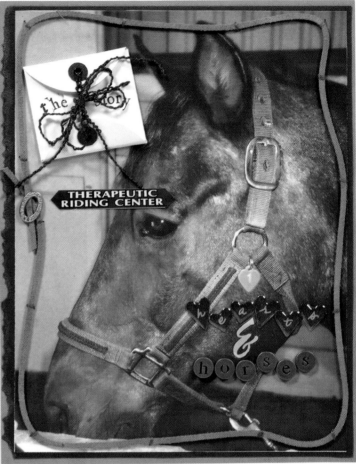

sheer joy!

Kathleen Paneitz created a highly visual layout about her daughter's physical therapy regimen designed to help her walk. Janae had been in conventional physical therapy for four years to learn how to bend her knees but had been having little success. After she started horseback therapy, she started bending her knees within a month. Kathleen used snapshots taken during the therapy sessions and an enlarged close-up photo of one of the horses on the layout, tucking her journaling in an envelope mounted on the right-hand page.

Design by Kathleen Paneitz

canine crack up

Sara Tumpane chose to highlight Casey's love of snow in this layout by using crackle medium to create the blue-and-white "snowy" background. Starting with heavy art paper, she painted the paper with medium blue paint and allowed it to dry. She then brushed on crackle medium and allowed it to dry according to the instructions on the bottle. A coat of white paint applied on top of the crackle medium reveals the blue paint below.

Design by Sara Tumpane

girl's best friend

After her children pleaded for months, Vivian Smith's sister gave in to their request for a dog. Buster quickly became a part of the family. Vivian wanted to document this, so she snapped this photo of her niece with Buster.

Vivian used a transparency to create a shadow-box style layout. Starting with the bottom layer, she matted the photo and mounted it on card stock printed with her journaling. Next, she made the frame from navy card stock and rolled back the inside edges, topping it with panoramic photos of grass. Vivian then printed the title on a transparency and outlined "Best Friend" in white ink to give it more impact. She attached the transparency to the back of the frame and used foam-core board to mount the frame onto the card stock background.

Design by Vivian Smith

Come on Cindy. Come on!
Never mind the beagle
puppy that torments you
and chases you all over
the house! Come on! I
promise Jackson wont
pull your tail! Come on!
You can come inside! I
have some nice kitty food
for you. So come inside
before the doggy gets it!
Come on Cindy. You
know you want to sleep
in Megan's room and
scratch her carpet all
night! We love you!
Come on kitty !!

KITTY KITTY

kitty kitty

Instead of creating a list of characteristics about her cat, Mary Ann Wise let these photos guide her journaling down a different path. After eight years, Mary Ann knows her cat's habits well, and she let her journaling reflect on a common activity—calling her cat to come closer.

Mary Ann got down to cat-eye level to take these striking photos. Using an enlarged photo and oversize mats helped to minimize distraction from the patterned paper background. A soft layer of vellum showcases the journaling and the die-cut title, while strips and circles of patterned paper create a cohesive design.

Design by Mary Ann Wise

focus on pets

Use these embellishments to finish a favorite page focusing on your beloved pet.

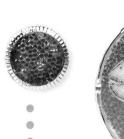

sophie girl tag

A square metal tag is the base of this embellishment. Top the tag with card stock and stickers. Add dangling charms and a ribbon to finish the look.

Design by Erin Terrell

fish and bubbles

To get a bubbly, glossy look, adhere a fish sticker to blue card stock; top with plenty of glaze, then add a layer of tiny clear beads. Let the glaze dry, and place the round tag around the fish. Pour another layer of glaze on top, let it dry, and trim off the excess card stock. Repeat the process for the bubbles, using conchos instead of a tag.

Design by Jennifer Wohlenberg

turtle

A large slide mount serves as a frame; green ink and embossing powder give the mount its sheen, and textured paper creates a bumpy look for the shell.

Design by Jennifer Wohlenberg

food dish

Brown beads make perfect dog food in this metal dish. Cut the dish shape from metal and emboss the design on it, stamping your dog's name. Adhere tiny beads for "food."

Design by Lori Bergmann

paw prints tag

Chalk the metal-rim tag and add black brads for the center of each paw print. Snap eyelets complete the paws. Add a chain and alphabet beads to complete the look.

Design by Shannon Landen

expressing
friendship

In the spirit of friendship, express your feelings by crafting special cards and gifts for those you care most about.

checkbook covers

A delightful checkbook cover will make paying bills a bit more pleasant for each recipient of these handcrafted gifts. For variation, Lori Bergmann suggests covering similarly sized calendars purchased at discount stores. Lori removed a checkbook cover from its protective plastic and used it as a pattern for cutting patterned paper inserts. She rubber-stamped a message and added die cuts and stickers to complete the designs, before slipping the artwork into their plastic covers.

Design by Lori Bergmann

friends and sisters frame

Charla Campbell painted a transparency to make a rough frame to enclose a photo. She punched a square from the center of a square transparency and brushed green paint around the opening. Then, she stamped the faint words on light green card stock, adhered the photo, and attached the transparency to the piece with eyelets at each corner. To complete the photo mat, she also lightly painted the edges of the bottom card stock and added a tag.

Design by Charla Campbell

my best friend card

Helen Naylor crafted this warm, fuzzy card from felt for a special friend. She layered the felt pieces and stitched a muzzle piece to the face with cream thread. She also stitched a nose and eyes with black floss for added interest. Felt has many advantages as an embellishment: It has a warm texture, doesn't fray when cut, and while it's thicker than card stock, a single layer doesn't add much bulk. Felt can be altered by using a wire brush to "fuzz" it up to make it look furry or antiqued by dipping it in tea or coffee. The pattern is on *page 62*.

Design by Helen Naylor

christmas photo mini album

Nichol Magouirk designed this mini album to preserve the many Christmas photos her family receives from friends each year. Nichol displays it during the holidays, and says it took only an afternoon to assemble.

She adhered the photos to the 6×6-inch pages and put them in order. Then she used sticker letters on the facing pages to identify the people in the photos. The front cover is also 6×6 inches, but the back cover is 7½×6 inches to allow for a fold-over flap. Nichol attached a bookplate to the front cover with mini brads, added a label for the title, and used stickers to denote the year. A punched card stock circle attached with a snap eyelet provides a closure fastener on each cover (place one on the folded flap); she threaded a fastening string through the hole in the back before attaching the eyelet. A Rollabind punch binds the pages and covers.

Design by Nichol Magouirk

FRIENDSHIP

...sharing special times with special friends...
on "the" special day!

friendship album

As each of Leslie Lightfoot's friends gets married, she collects photos. "I decided it would be nice to do a collection of pages of my favorite photos from each friend's wedding," Leslie says. "This way, all my favorites are in one album, and when we all get together, we can look it over and reminisce."

Leslie wanted a soft, romantic look for the album, so she used black-and-white photos, a monochromatic color scheme, and layers of tulle.

The title page, *opposite,* includes a quotation about friendship printed on vellum. A cropped wedding bouquet photo is matted with mesh. Leslie machine-stitched a strip of embossed paper into place using white thread. The matted photo was adhered to the page and the vellum journaling was stitched in place on top.

For the table of contents, *above left,* Leslie stitched strips of embossed paper to white card stock. She printed each couple's names and wedding dates on vellum, cut the sheet into narrow strips, and sewed them to the page. Varied lengths and alignment lend an informal look. Cropped photos complete the page.

To create a dramatic look for the interior pages, *above right* and *below left* and *right,* Leslie thought in layers. Woven mesh and a large square of vellum top embossed paper. (To hide the adhesive tabs holding the sheets in place until she stitched them, Leslie positioned the tabs where she knew they'd be hidden by the photos.) After adhering the vellum, she added the photos and then topped each photo and vellum with two layers of tulle with a window cut to reveal a portion of the image. She stitched the tulle in place around the edges of the photograph and the vellum. A printed caption, a quotation, and a few buttons finish the pages.

Design by Leslie Lightfoot

friends are flowers

A painted flowerpot filled with moss or posies and topped with a clever quotation or saying makes a delightful anytime gift for a special friend. This friendship "pick" starts with a favorite photo mounted on layered papers. Marker-drawn flowers, die cuts, and an appropriate hand-written quote finish it. Painting the pot to match makes this gift a sure favorite.

Design by Vicki Breslin

happy birthday, my dear friend card

Delicate daisies are an ideal choice to celebrate a spring birthday. This card features daisy-pattern paper muted by a vellum overlay that bears the printed message. The three-dimensional daisy accents are made by punching six daisies from white card stock. Two daisies are stacked to make a double flower. Each double flower is positioned on the card; a hole is punched in the center through the vellum, patterned paper, and the card front. A brad holds each flower in place.

Design by Kathleen Paneitz

'sew'-long invitation

This invitation clearly and concisely says it all in black and white: It's time for good friends to get together again. The clever design is easy enough that you can reproduce plenty of them in an evening. Print on and layer pretty papers, then accent with appropriate embellishments. Here, the binding tape and button continue the sewing theme.

Design by Vicki Breslin

patterns

NATURE

Exploring Nature
page 35

Mt. Lemmon Snow
page 39

①

②

③

PRESSURE

→ RELEASE

My Best Friend Card
page 56

Aa Bb Cc Dd
Ee Ff Gg Hh Ii
Jj Kk Ll Mm
Nn Oo Pp Qq
Rr Ss Tt Uu Vv
Ww Xx Yy Zz

Better Homes and Gardens®
Creative Collection™

Editorial Director
Gayle Goodson Butler

Editor-in-Chief
Beverly Rivers

Executive Editor Karman Wittry Hotchkiss

Art Director **Contributing Editorial Manager**
Brenda Drake Lesch Heidi Palkovic

Contributing Editor Kathy Roth Eastman
Contributing Design Director Tracy DeVenney
Contributing Graphic Designer Wendy Musgrave
Copy Chief Mary Heaton
Contributing Copy Editor Nancy Dietz
Proofreader Dana Schmidt
Administrative Assistant Lori Eggers

Senior Vice President
Bob Mate

Publishing Group President
Jack Griffin

CORPORATION

Chairman and CEO William T. Kerr
President and COO Stephen M. Lacy

In Memoriam
E. T. Meredith III (1933–2003)